NO PEANUTS, NO PROBLEM!

Easy and Delicious Nut-Free Recipes
for Kids With Allergies

by **KATRINA JORGENSEN**

CONSULTANT
Amy Durkan MS, RDN, CDN
Nutrition Research Manager
Mount Sinai Medical Center
New York, NY

CAPSTONE PRESS
a capstone imprint

Edge Books are published by Capstone Press,
1710 Roe Crest Drive, North Mankato, Minnesota 56003
www.mycapstone.com

Library of Congress Cataloging-in-Publication Data
Cataloging-in-Publication data is on file with the Library of Congress.
ISBN 978-1-4914-8054-0 (library binding)
ISBN 978-1-4914-8059-5 (eBook PDF)

Editorial Credits
Anna Butzer, editor; Heidi Thompson, designer; Morgan Walters, media researcher;
Sarah Schuette, food stylist; Kathy McColley, production specialist

Design Elements
Shutterstock: avian, design element, Katerina Kirilova, design element, Lena Pan, design
element, Marco Govel, design element, mexrix, design element, Sabina Pittak, design
element, STILLFX, design element, swatchandsoda, design element

Photography by Capstone Studio: Karon Dubke

Editor's note:
Capstone cannot ensure that any food is allergen-free. The only way to be sure a food is
safe is to read all labels carefully, every time. Cross-contamination is also a risk for those
with food allergies. Please call food companies to make sure their manufacturing processes
avoid cross-contamination. Also, always be sure to clean hands, surfaces, and tools
before cooking.

Printed and bound in the USA.
009675F16

TABLE OF CONTENTS

SESAME GRANOLA BARS........................6

APPLE MUFFINS............................8

BANANA-CHOCOLATE CRÈME PANCAKES.......10

APPLE SANDWICH..........................12

THAI CHICKEN SALAD.......................14

PUMPKIN SEED PESTO PASTA................16

HONEY GARLIC CHICKEN WINGS.............18

SESAME GREEN BEANS......................20

BBQ ROASTED CHICKPEAS..................22

SUNFLOWER BUTTER COOKIES...............24

CHOCOLATE SUNFLOWER CUPS..............26

NO-NUT BRITTLE..........................28

STRAWBERRY-AVOCADO POWER SMOOTHIE...30

GLOSSARY........................32

READ MORE.....................32

INTERNET SITES................32

WHAT IS A FOOD ALLERGY?

Our bodies are armed with immune systems. It's the immune system's job to fight infections, viruses, and invaders. Sometimes the immune system identifies a certain food as one of these invaders and attacks it. While our immune system fights, a chemical response is triggered and causes an allergic reaction. Reactions vary greatly from a mild skin irritation to having trouble breathing. Any time you feel you are having a reaction, tell an adult immediately.

The best way to avoid having an allergic reaction is to be aware of what you are eating. Be careful not to consume the allergen that affects you. If you are not sure if that allergen is in a food, ask an adult or read the ingredient label of the food container before eating. Unfortunately, allergens can sometimes be hard to identify in an ingredient list. Check out http://www.foodallergy.org for a full list of hidden peanut and tree nut terms.

Avoiding food allergens can be hard to manage, especially when they are found in so many of our favorite foods. This cookbook will take you on a culinary journey to explore many of the dishes you've had to avoid because of a peanut or tree nut allergy.

Kitchen Safety

A safe kitchen is a fun kitchen! Always start your recipes with clean hands, surfaces, and tools. Wash your hands and any tools you may use in future steps of a recipe, especially when handling raw meat. Make sure you have an adult nearby to help you with any task you don't feel comfortable doing, such as cutting vegetables or carrying hot pans.

ALLERGY ALERTS AND TIPS

Have other food allergies? No problem.
Check out the list at the end of each recipe
for substitutions for other common allergens.
Look out for other cool tips and ideas too!

CONVERSIONS

			Fahrenheit (°F)	Celsius (°C)
1/4 teaspoon	1.25 grams or milliliters			
1/2 teaspoon	2.5 g or mL		325°	160°
1 teaspoon	5 g or mL		350°	180°
1 tablespoon	15 g or mL		375°	190°
1/4 cup	57 g (dry) or 60 mL (liquid)		400°	200°
1/3 cup	75 g (dry) or 80 mL (liquid)		425°	220°
1/2 cup	114 g (dry) or 125 mL (liquid)		450°	230°
2/3 cup	150 g (dry) or 160 mL (liquid)			
3/4 cup	170 g (dry) or 175 mL (liquid)			
1 cup	227 g (dry) or 240 mL (liquid)			
1 quart	950 mL			

SESAME GRANOLA BARS

Get ready for granola on the go! Nuts are almost always found in granola, but you can make homemade bars that are nut-free. Crunchy and delicious, these granola bars will satisfy your hunger when you're out and about.

Prep Time: 30 minutes
  (20 minutes inactive)

Cook Time: 15 minutes

Makes 12 bars

Ingredients

2 cups rolled oats

1 cup pitted dates

¼ cup honey

¼ cup sunflower butter

1 tablespoon tahini
(sesame seed paste)

2 tablespoons sunflower seeds

2 tablespoons flax seeds

3 tablespoons sesame seeds

Tools

large baking sheet

measuring cups/spoons

food processor

large mixing bowl

8 x 8-inch (20 x 20-centimeter)
baking dish

parchment paper

chef's knife

Allergen Alert!

Many dates and dried fruits
are manufactured with nuts.
Check labels carefully, and call
the manufacturer for details.

Make sure your rolled oats are certified
wheat-free if you avoid wheat.

1. Preheat oven to 350°F. Evenly spread out the rolled oats on a large baking sheet. Place in the oven for 15 minutes, or until golden brown.

2. While the oats bake, place the dates in the food processor. Blend on high until the dates look like a ball of dough. Add the honey, sunflower butter, and tahini and pulse until well blended.

3. Place the toasted oats and all seeds in the large bowl. Carefully remove the blade from the food processor and pour in the date mixture.

4. Use your hands to squish the mixture until the oats and seeds are coated well.

5. Wash your hands. Line the bottom of the baking dish with parchment paper.

6. Empty the contents of the mixing bowl into the baking dish. Use your hands to press the mixture flat, making one large square.

7. Place the dish in a refrigerator for at least 20 minutes to harden.

8. Slice into 12 bars.

9. Wrap in parchment paper and place in the refrigerator for up to one week.

CHEF'S TIP

Keep your bars for a longer period of time
by placing them in your freezer. Put one in
your lunchbox in the morning and it will be
perfectly thawed for your midday meal!

APPLE MUFFINS

Grab the muffin tin and get ready to bake! These sweet treats are a perfect nut-free addition to the breakfast table. You'll fall in love with these fluffy muffins overflowing with flavor!

Prep Time: 15 minutes

Cook Time: 30 minutes

Makes 12 muffins

Ingredients

2 tablespoons flaxseed meal

¼ cup water

1 Granny Smith apple

2 cups all-purpose flour

½ cup sugar

1 ½ tablespoons pumpkin pie spice

1 teaspoon baking soda

1 teaspoon baking powder

1 ½ cups applesauce

½ cup sunflower oil

Tools

standard muffin tin

12 muffin liners

measuring cups/spoons

2 mixing bowls

whisk

peeler

cutting board

chef's knife

spoon

toothpick

Allergen Alert!

If you're avoiding wheat, make sure you use a wheat-free flour mix instead of all-purpose flour.

1. Preheat oven to 350°F. Line muffin tin with liners and set aside.

2. In a mixing bowl, combine the flaxseed meal and water. Stir with a whisk. Allow to sit for at least five minutes.

3. Peel and core the apple, and then cut into small cubes. Set aside.

4. In the unused mixing bowl, add the remaining dry ingredients. Stir to combine.

5. Add applesauce and sunflower oil to the flaxseed mix. Whisk to combine, then pour over the flour mixture.

6. Stir until most lumps are gone.

7. Drop in the apples. Stir until coated.

8. Fill each of the muffin cups two-thirds full.

9. Place in the oven for about 30 minutes. Insert a toothpick in the center of a muffin. If it comes out clean, the muffins are done. Remove muffins from the oven and allow to cool slightly before serving.

10. Store leftovers in an airtight container at room temperature for up to one week.

CHEF'S TIP

Want to add another flavor into the mix? Swap the applesauce for 1 ¾ cups pumpkin puree.

BANANA-CHOCOLATE CRÈME
PANCAKES

Bananas + chocolate = YUM! Hazelnuts are an ingredient in chocolate crème, but you can get the same taste and texture with sunflower butter. Whip up a sweet pancake breakfast that your family will love!

Prep Time: 10 minutes

Cook Time: 10 minutes

Makes 8–10 pancakes

Ingredients

Chocolate Crème

½ cup sunflower butter

2 tablespoons cocoa powder

2 tablespoons honey

Banana Pancakes

3 bananas

1 ½ cups all-purpose flour

1 cup water

1 teaspoon baking powder

¼ teaspoon salt

cooking spray

Tools

2 mixing bowls

measuring cups/spoons

2 forks

chef's knife

cutting board

whisk

skillet

ladle

spatula

Allergen Alert!

Cocoa and chocolate are often manufactured with nuts. Check labels carefully, and call the manufacturer for details.

Replace the all-purpose flour with wheat-free flour mix if you're avoiding wheat!

1. In a mixing bowl, combine all crème ingredients. Mix well with a fork. Set aside.

2. Peel the bananas, and slice two of them into ½-inch (1.3-cm) rounds. Set aside. Mash the last banana well with a fork.

3. Scrape the mashed banana into a second mixing bowl. Add the flour, water, baking powder, and salt. Whisk until most lumps are gone.

4. Place the skillet on a burner set to medium heat.

5. When the pan is hot, add cooking spray to the surface. Then scoop ½ cup of batter onto the hot pan.

6. Allow to cook until bubbles appear around the edges.

7. Using the spatula, flip the pancake. Cook until golden brown.

8. Remove the pancake from the heat and place on a plate. Repeat steps 5 through 8 until all batter is gone.

9. To serve, spread 2 tablespoons of the chocolate crème on a pancake, followed by 6–7 slices of banana.

10. Serve immediately. Leftover chocolate crème can be stored in the refrigerator for up to two weeks.

CHEF'S TIP

Don't want to monkey around with bananas to? Slice up 1 cup (8 ounces) of strawberries instead for a sweet alternative!

APPLE SANDWICH

Make your own sandwich—without bread or peanut butter! Cast aside the bread and use apples instead. Sunflower butter takes over the role of peanut butter so you can be nut-free without sacrificing the flavor.

Prep Time: 5 minutes

Cook Time: 1 minute

Makes 2 apple sandwiches

Ingredients

1 apple—your favorite kind

1 lemon

4 tablespoons sunflower butter

2 tablespoons of your choice of topping: rolled oats, raisins, pumpkin seeds, sesame seeds, or jam

Tools

cutting board

chef's knife

small round cookie cutter

measuring spoons

butter knife

1. Carefully cut the top and bottom off the apple, about ½-inch (1.3-cm) thick. Enjoy those pieces later!

2. Cut the remaining apple into four even slices for making two sandwiches. Set aside.

3. Using the round cookie cutter, cut the cores out of each slice and discard.

4. Cut the lemon in half. Gently squeeze a few drops of juice on both sides of the apple slices.

5. Spread 2 tablespoons of sunflower butter on two of the apple slices.

6. Sprinkle or spread your choice of topping over the sunflower butter.

7. Place the plain apple slices over the sunflower butter slices to make a sandwich.

8. Eat immediately, or store in an airtight container for up to one day.

Allergen Alert!

Dried fruits, such as raisins, and seeds are often manufactured with nuts. Check labels carefully, and call the manufacturer for details.

If you're going to put rolled oats on your sandwich, make sure you get a wheat-free version if you're avoiding wheat.

CHEF'S TIP

Why put lemon on your apples? When you slice an apple, you expose the pulp to oxygen that causes it to turn brown. It's OK to eat apple slices that have turned brown (within a day or two of slicing). The acid in lemon juice forms a protective barrier that keeps your apples looking perfectly fresh!

THAI CHICKEN SALAD

How do you get a nutty flavor without the nuts? With sesame seeds! Peanuts are a staple ingredient in Thai food, but you won't miss them in this crunchy salad topped with a tangy dressing.

Prep Time: 20 minutes

Cook Time: 15 minutes

Serves 4

Ingredients

Dressing

¼ cup sunflower butter

2 teaspoons tahini
 (sesame seed paste)

2 tablespoons lime juice

3 tablespoons olive oil

1 tablespoon coconut aminos

3 tablespoons honey

1 tablespoon crushed garlic

1 tablespoon crushed ginger

½ teaspoon salt

¼ cup fresh cilantro

Salad

1 pound (16 oz) boneless,
 skinless chicken thighs

1 teaspoon salt

½ teaspoon pepper

2 tablespoons olive oil

1 bell pepper

1 cucumber

4 cups coleslaw mix

1 green onion

2 teaspoons sesame seeds

Tools

blender

measuring cups/spoons

cutting board

chef's knife

skillet

serving bowl

tongs

1. In a blender, combine all of the dressing ingredients. Blend on high until smooth.

2. Cut the chicken into bite-sized pieces. Sprinkle with salt and pepper.

3. Wash your hands, cutting board, and chef's knife after you have finished handling the chicken.

4. Heat the olive oil in a skillet over medium-high heat and add the chicken.

5. Cook the chicken on all sides, about eight to 10 minutes, or until no longer pink in the center. Set aside.

6. Cut the stem off the bell pepper, and then cut down the center. Carefully pull out the seeds and discard. Cut the pepper into small pieces and set aside.

7. Slice the cucumber into ¼-inch (0.6-cm) rounds and set aside.

8. To assemble the salad, place the coleslaw mix, bell pepper, cucumber, and chicken in a serving bowl.

9. Drizzle half of the dressing over the salad. Toss with tongs to coat all of the ingredients.

10. Add more dressing if necessary, then sprinkle with sesame seeds.

11. Serve immediately with leftover dressing on the side, if desired.

Allergen Alert!

Although sesame isn't considered one of the top eight food allergens, it's a very common allergy. Leave the sesame seeds off if you're allergic to them.

PUMPKIN SEED PESTO
PASTA

You may get tongue-tied trying to say this recipe name, but you can reward your taste buds with this light and fresh pasta. Pesto is usually made with pine nuts, but pumpkin seeds allow you to keep nuts out of the recipe.

Prep Time: 5 minutes

Cook Time: 15 minutes

Serves 4

Ingredients

1 gallon water

2 tablespoons salt

8 ounces pasta, any shape

Pesto

2 cups fresh basil leaves

¼ cup extra virgin olive oil

¼ cup pumpkin seeds

2 garlic cloves

½ teaspoon lemon juice

¼ cup shredded Parmesan
  cheese

½ teaspoon salt

¼ teaspoon ground black pepper

Tools

large pot

measuring cups/spoons

blender

colander

serving bowl

tongs

1. Place water in a large pot with salt. Set pot on a burner set to high.

2. When the water begins to boil, add the pasta. Reduce heat to a low boil. Cook according to package directions.

3. Combine all pesto ingredients in a blender. Blend on high until smooth. Set aside.

4. When the pasta is cooked, carefully drain into a colander.

5. Transfer pasta to a serving bowl and add half of the pesto.

6. Toss gently with tongs until the pasta is coated. Add more pesto if desired.

7. Serve immediately. Store leftover pesto in an airtight container in a refrigerator for up to three days.

Allergen Alert!

Do you need to avoid dairy?
Trade the Parmesan cheese for
equal parts nutritional yeast.

Egg-free or wheat-free pasta can
be used in place of regular pasta.

HONEY GARLIC
CHICKEN WINGS

Want something finger-lickin' good but also easy to make? These sticky and sweet glazed chicken wings are sure to please. Whether you're serving them for a jazzed-up weeknight meal or a tantalizing party appetizer, these crispy wings with bold flavor will be the star!

Prep Time: 15 minutes

Cook Time: 2 hours 40 minutes
(2 ½ hours inactive)

Serves 4 as a meal, 8 as an appetizer

Ingredients

2 tablespoons crushed garlic

¼ cup olive oil

¼ cup honey

2 tablespoons soy sauce

2 tablespoons brown sugar

1 teaspoon cornstarch

2 pounds (32 oz) bone-in chicken wings (about 24 wings)

1 teaspoon salt

½ teaspoon black pepper

1 tablespoon sesame seeds

Tools

measuring cups/spoons

medium mixing bowl

whisk

cutting board

paper towels

tongs

2 quart slow cooker

large baking sheet

parchment paper

ladle

1. Combine the first six ingredients in a medium mixing bowl. Whisk until smooth. Set aside.

2. Place the chicken wings on a cutting board and pat dry with paper towels.

3. Sprinkle salt and pepper on both sides of the wings. Pat with hands to make sure it sticks. Wash your hands when done.

4. Use tongs to place the wings in the bottom of the slow cooker. Pour sauce over top. Stir to coat.

5. Put the lid on the slow cooker and set on high for two and a half hours.

6. When the wings are almost done, preheat oven to 450°F. Line a large baking sheet with parchment paper and set aside.

7. When the wings are done, use tongs to place them on the baking sheet about ½ inch (1.3 cm) apart.

8. Place in the oven for about 10 minutes, or until the skin is slightly crispy and browned.

9. Ladle the remaining sauce over the wings. Toss to coat.

10. Sprinkle with sesame seeds and serve hot.

CHEF'S TIP

You don't want to use chicken wings? You can make this recipe with chicken thighs or drumsticks. Just add an hour of cooking time to your slow cooker (3 ½ hours, instead of 2 ½).

SESAME GREEN
BEANS

Add some flair to the dinner table with Asian-inspired green beans. A play on green beans almondine, this dish replaces almonds with sesame seeds for a delicious crunch.

Prep Time: 5 minutes

Cook Time: 5 minutes

Serves 4

Ingredients

1 16-ounce microwavable bag
of fresh green beans

2 teaspoons olive oil

1 teaspoon toasted sesame oil

1 teaspoon coconut aminos

1 teaspoon honey

1 tablespoon sesame seeds

Tools

measuring spoons

skillet

tongs

wooden spoon

serving bowl

Allergen Alert!

You can leave the sesame seeds off
if you have a sesame allergy.

1. Cook green beans in the microwave according to directions on package. Set aside to cool slightly before opening.

2. In a skillet, heat the olive oil over medium-high heat.

3. Carefully open the bag. Watch out for hot steam. Pour the green beans into the skillet.

4. Using tongs, toss the green beans around to coat with oil.

5. Add the sesame oil, coconut aminos, and honey.

6. Stir the green beans quickly as the sauce begins to slightly thicken.

7. Transfer the green beans to a serving bowl. Sprinkle with sesame seeds.

8. Toss gently with tongs to coat all of the beans. Serve hot.

CHEF'S TIP

You can use any green vegetable you like
for this recipe, such as broccoli, spinach,
peas, or asparagus!

BBQ ROASTED
CHICKPEAS

Combine a smoky BBQ flavor with the crunch of roasted chickpeas and you get a tasty, southern-inspired snack! These chickpeas are not only delicious but they are also a healthy treat loaded with protein.

Prep Time: 40 minutes
(30 minutes inactive)

Cook Time: 45 minutes

Makes 4 cups

Ingredients

2 15-ounce cans chickpeas
   (also known as garbanzo beans)

2 teaspoons brown sugar

2 teaspoons salt

2 teaspoons garlic powder

½ teaspoon ground white pepper

1 teaspoon dry mustard

½ teaspoon cayenne pepper

½ teaspoon cumin

2 teaspoons smoked paprika

2 tablespoons olive oil

Tools

baking sheet

parchment paper

can opener

colander

paper towels

mixing bowl

measuring spoons

spatula

Allergens Eradicated!

No major food allergens found here!

1. Preheat oven to 400°F. Line a baking sheet with parchment paper and set aside.

2. Open the cans of chickpeas and empty them into the colander.

3. Keeping the chickpeas in the colander, rinse with cool water.

4. Line a clean surface with paper towels and spread the chickpeas on top.

5. Allow to sit for about 30 minutes to dry almost completely.

6. While the chickpeas dry, make your flavoring. Combine remaining ingredients in a mixing bowl. Stir until smooth.

7. When the chickpeas are mostly dry, transfer them to the mixing bowl. Stir to coat evenly.

8. Spread the chickpeas evenly on the baking sheet.

9. Bake in the oven for about 45 minutes, or until golden brown and hardened.

10. Remove from oven and allow to cool slightly before serving.

11. Store leftovers in an airtight container for up to three days.

SUNFLOWER BUTTER
COOKIES

With the help of sunflower butter, you can make a nut-free dessert with a nutty flavor! Crunchy on the outside and soft on the inside, these simple cookies are made with only five ingredients.

Prep Time: 10 minutes

Cook Time: 10 minutes

Makes 1 dozen cookies

24

Ingredients

2 tablespoons flaxseed meal

¼ cup water

1 cup sunflower butter

¾ cup sugar

¼ cup brown sugar

Tools

baking sheet

parchment paper

measuring cups/spoons

mixing bowl

spatula

cooling rack

Allergens Eradicated!

No major food allergens found here!

1. Preheat the oven to 350°F. Line a baking sheet with parchment paper.

2. In a mixing bowl, combine the flaxseed meal and water. Stir and allow to sit for five minutes before continuing.

3. Add the sunflower butter, sugar, and brown sugar to the flaxseed mixture. Stir well until it begins to thicken, about one minute.

4. Divide the dough into 12 equally sized pieces. Roll into balls between your palms.

5. Place the dough balls on the baking sheet, evenly spaced. Leave at least 2 inches (5.1 cm) of space between the balls.

6. Use your palm to flatten each dough ball slightly.

7. Place in the oven and bake for about 10 minutes.

8. Remove from oven and allow to cool for five minutes before transferring to a cooling rack.

9. Serve warm or at room temperature and store leftovers in an airtight container for up to three days.

CHEF'S TIP

Are you craving chocolate? Add chocolate chips to the mix in step 3! Make sure the chocolate chips you use are free of allergens.

CHOCOLATE SUNFLOWER
CUPS

Give the traditional peanut butter cup a nut-free makeover! Delight your taste buds by combining smooth milk chocolate and creamy sunflower butter into one delectable, bite-sized dessert.

Prep Time: 1 hour 10 minutes
(1 hour inactive)

Makes 1 dozen cups

Ingredients

cooking spray

½ cup sunflower butter

¼ cup confectioner's sugar

¼ teaspoon salt

1 cup semi-sweet chocolate chips

Tools

mini muffin tin

12 mini muffin liners

mixing bowl

measuring cups/spoons

spatula

microwave-safe bowl

Allergen Alert!

Chocolate chips can contain or be manufactured with soy, nuts, and dairy. Make sure to check that the chocolate chips you use are free of allergens.

1. Place 12 mini muffin liners in a mini muffin tin. Spray a small amount of cooking spray in each liner and set aside.

2. In a mixing bowl, combine the sunflower butter, confectioner's sugar, and salt. Mix until thickened. Add more confectioner's sugar if needed.

3. Divide the dough into 12 pieces. Roll each piece between your palms to make 12 small balls. Set aside.

4. In a microwave-safe bowl, melt the chocolate chips by cooking on medium for two minutes. Stir, and then cook on medium an additional minute.

5. To assemble, spread a small amount of chocolate in each liner, followed by a sunflower butter ball. Top with remaining chocolate, until the ball is covered.

6. Place in refrigerator to cool for at least one hour.

7. Store leftovers in refrigerator for up to one week, or in freezer for up to one month.

BRITTLE

What do you get when you take the peanuts out of peanut brittle? No-nut brittle! Pumpkin seeds add to the crunch in this caramel-flavored candy.

Prep Time: 10 minutes

Cook Time: 2 ½ hours
(2 hours inactive)

Serves 10–12

Ingredients

½ cup white sugar

½ cup brown sugar

4 ounces corn syrup

1 cup pumpkin seeds

1 teaspoon butter

½ teaspoon vanilla extract

½ teaspoon maple extract

1 teaspoon baking soda

Tools

8 x 8-inch (20 x 20-cm)
  baking dish

parchment paper

measuring cups/spoons

large microwave-safe mixing bowl

spatula

1. Line a baking dish with parchment paper and set aside.

2. In a mixing bowl, combine the white sugar, brown sugar, and corn syrup. Microwave on high for three minutes.

3. Carefully remove from microwave and add the pumpkin seeds. Stir to combine.

4. Return bowl to microwave and cook on high for an additional three minutes.

5. Remove bowl from the microwave. Add the butter, vanilla extract, and maple extract. Stir carefully.

6. Microwave on high for one minute.

7. Remove from microwave and add the baking soda. Stir to combine.

8. Pour into prepared baking dish, and allow to sit for at least two hours to cool.

9. When cooled, break into pieces for serving.

10. Store leftovers in an airtight container at room temperature for up to one week.

CHEF'S TIP

Don't mess with the crunch! Replace
pumpkin seeds with other seeds such
as sesame or sunflower seeds.

STRAWBERRY-AVOCADO POWER

SMOOTHIE

Looking for a quick-and-easy smoothie that's both healthy and nut-free? Like nuts, avocados are rich in B vitamins. Add in strawberries, and you have a delicious, nutritious drink.

Prep Time: 5 minutes

Makes 1 smoothie

Ingredients

½ avocado

½ cup frozen strawberries

1 frozen banana

½ cup milk

1 tablespoon honey

Tools

cutting board

chef's knife

spoon

measuring cups/spoons

blender

Allergen Alert!

Make sure you select a milk
that meets your dietary needs,
or use your favorite fruit juice.

1. Carefully slice the avocado in half and remove the pit.

2. Scoop half of the avocado flesh into the blender, followed by the frozen strawberries, banana, milk, and honey.

3. Blend on high until smooth.

4. Pour into a serving glass, and serve immediately with a large straw.

CHEF'S TIP

Wishing for a thicker smoothie? Add a handful of
crushed ice to your blender for a triple-thick delight!

Freezing your own fruit is fast and easy.

Strawberries: Wash and dry the strawberries well.
Cut the stems off the tops of the strawberries,
then slice each lengthwise.

Bananas: Peel the bananas and
slice them into ½-inch (1.3-cm) rounds.

To freeze your fruits: Line a baking sheet
with parchment paper and place strawberries
and banana slices on it, flat sides down.
Freeze for three hours and then transfer to
a freezer-safe zip-top bag.

GLOSSARY

assemble—to put all the parts of something together

blend—to mix together, sometimes using a blender

boil—to heat until large bubbles form on top of a liquid; the boiling point for water is 212°F (100°C)

consume—to eat or drink something

discard—to throw something away because it is not needed

drizzle—to let a substance fall in small drops

mash—to smash a soft food into a lumpy mixture

pit—the single central seed or stone of certain fruits

pulp—the soft juicy or fleshy part of a fruit or vegetable

slice—to cut into thin pieces with a knife

thaw—to bring frozen food to room temperature

whisk—to stir a mixture rapidly until it's smooth

READ MORE

Besel, Jen. *Sweet Tooth! No-Bake Desserts to Make and Devour.* North Mankato, Minn.: Capstone Press, 2015.

Cook, Deanna F. *Cooking Class: 57 Fun Recipes Kids Will Love to Make (and Eat!).* North Adams, MA: Storey Publishing, 2015.

McAneney, Caitie. *Peanut and Other Food Allergies.* Let's Talk About It. New York: PowerKids Press, 2015.

INTERNET SITES

Use FactHound to find Internet sites related to this book. All of the sites on FactHound have been researched by our staff.

Here's all you do:

Visit *www.facthound.com*

Type in this code: 9781491480540